THE ULTIMATE JEWISH CARTOON BOOK

by Neil Kerber

First published in Great Britain in 2009 by
JR Books, 10 Greenland Street, London NW1 0ND
www.jrbooks.com

A catalogue record for this book is available from the British Library.

ISBN 978-1-906779-55-9

1 3 5 7 9 10 8 6 4 2

Printed by MPG Books, Bodmin, Cornwall

IT'S HER FIRST "SHRUG"!!!
I'LL GET THE CAMERA!!!
OY!

Great Jewish boxers no:356729

Stanley "Lemon tea" Pinkus

The oldest ever heavyweight champion, "Lemon tea", went on to fight well into his eighties, but finally had to retire when every punch he took was below the belt.

TABLE PLAN
I WORK IN A DNA LAB, CREATING NEW LIFE!
DO YOU MAKE A LIVING?

Jewish globe

THE CHOSEN EPISODE 1

Yentas don't like to rush relationships

"I'm sorry bubbelah, I never pinch a man's cheeks on a first date!"

Jewish monsters

"Frankenstein, you say? You're not related to Yettie and Mitzy Frankenstein? . . . oh no, that's Finkelstein!!!"

Moses's wife goes into labour

"It's my wife . . . her waters are parting!!!"

*"Mum, Dad, this is my new boyfriend Irwin.
He carries the Torah in his shul!"*

Yiddishe mice

"Sorry to trouble you bubbelah, have you got anything softer? I'm hoping to make a cheesecake!"

"Actually I'm not really Jewish, I converted!"

Christmas with the Three Wisemans

2 million B.J.
(Before Jews)

Advertisement

70s Hassidics.

Deli
I'LL HAVE SOME FISHBALLS, SHMALTZ HERRING, EGG 'N' ONION, SMOKED SALMON, AND GEFILTE FISH. ...I THINK THAT'S EVERYTHING!
WHAT AM I, CHOPPED LIVER?

Two Jews, stuck together in a lifeboat, stranded at sea for days . . . what would they say to each other?

Jewish Supermodels ("Jewpermodels")

"I starve myself for the sake of my career. I haven't eaten for 3 minutes!!!"

THE CHOSEN EPISODE 2

Great Jewish boxers no:562894

Irwin "Kid" Kiddelshnoff

In the days when fights lasted for ever, welterweight champion "Kid" Kiddelshnoff once defeated "Sugar Ray" Sugar in a world title contest that lasted for 28 weeks, 3 days and 7 hours. During the fight, he also managed to complete a couple of crucial business deals, bring his accounts up to date, and host his son's BarMitzvah.

"Son, when a young Jewish boy reaches 13, he becomes a man!!!"

"Darling, it can never work out between us. You're an alien from a distant galaxy, and my parents want me to meet someone Jewish!"

"Bad hair day!"

CAFE
BUT I THOUGHT "A GLASS OF O.J." MEANT "ORANGE JUICE"!!!
NO...... "OLD JEW"

Controversial modern art

DAMIEN HIRST's PICKLED SHEEP:

SHLOYMIE GLITZEL's PICKLED HERRING:

Shlaparazzi.

Doctor Dolittle shmoozes with the animals . . .

I HATE THE WAY JEWS ARE STEREOTYPED FOR THE SAKE OF COMEDY !!!
ME TOO! OY VAY MORE CHEESECAKE BUBBELAH?

Cannibal Jewish mothers

"Look at you . . . you look so thin . . .
you should eat me!!!"

"Which wine do you recommend to go with a nagging Yenta?"

"Me? . . . oh I'm just the awkward guy you always get stuck with at Jewish weddings!"

OY VAY!... EASY WITH THE SPADE BUBBELAH!!!
IT'S NICE TO FIND OUR JEWISH ROOTS!

"It's a blessing in disguise!"

Bergman of Alcatraz

GEFILTE
FISH

PSSST.........
HEY GORGEOUS,
D'YOU WANNA
GO OUT FOR
DINNER
TONIGHT ?
SORRY,
I'M STAYING IN
TO WASH
MY CARROT !

COMPLIMENTARY MEDICINE
NICE TOCHES!
THANKS!

Rarely ever mentioned, Cupid's mother was in fact Jewish . . .

"One minute I'm swimming along happily in the Red Sea . . .
the next thing I know, everything starts parting!!!"

Door to door Jewish parent

"Good morning Miss. Can I interest you in my son Howard? He's a lovely looking boy, don't you think?"

"Excuse me Sir, have you thought about head cover?"

New York 1873

Irwin Bagel makes an important suggestion

"Hey Morry, why don't you sell those outer 'ring-shaped' bits instead of throwing them away?!!"

ALWAYS COMPETING WITH EVERYBODY! YOU HAD TO GO AND BUY THE BIGGEST MEZUZAH!!! NOW WE'RE TRAPPED!!! HARVEY, YOU'RE A SHMOK!!!

GENTILE MEADOWS
GOLF CLUB
NO JEWS
IT'S NOT A ANTISEMITIC THING... WE JUST DON'T HAVE ANY RESTAURANTS HERE!
OY!!!

Goldzilla

HMM......
I COULD EAT A CAR PARK,
AND A SCHOOL PLAYGROUND....
.... BUT THEN I SHOULDN'T
HAVE CAKE!..

Jewish mother genetic food cloning scientists . . .

The Jewish princess and the frog

"So what car do you drive?"

The Invisible Man
(Yiddishe version)

Why Middle East peace talks often break down

"I can do you a nice chop. And also some meat for your dinner!"

Gefilte fishing

"Don't do it it Laurence . . . it's a trap!!!"

Early Jews

HOW GLOBAL WARMING IS AFFECTING JEWS

"It's an accountant!!!"

The Headless Horseman goes to synagogue

"Excuse me, would you mind covering your neck?"

Meanwhile, at Jewish auntie school . . .

"Right, Batman, you round up all evil, Superman, you save the world . . . and Goldman, you get the bagels!"

"Don't go out dressed like that . . . what are you, a meshuggenah?!!"

Jewish grandma horticulturalists

"Haven't you grown!!!"

Old Jewish proverb says:

"If a tree falls in the forest and no-one is around to hear it . . . why should I get involved? Trees are not my thing. What does a Jew know about trees?"

*"So that's the food and the band sorted . . .
now let's have a flick through* Renta Yenta *. . ."*

Famous Jewish crooners No.435672

Sammy "The Shmooze" Silkstein

The most popular member of the notorious "Shlap Pack", Sammy delighted Las Vegas audiences for decades with his beautiful tones and exciting dancing. However, his strong association with Jewish gangsters led to several arrests and public disgrace, culminating in him losing his synagogue membership. Such humiliation led to a failed suicide attempt in 1994, when he tried overdosing on fishballs. Hasn't been seen since,but you can sometimes smell him singing.

"And do you, Lorraine Rachel Hershenbloom, take Irving Saul Pinkel's credit card, to have and to spend on dresses and facial saunas, so long as you both shall live . . ."

Jewish martial arts

"First you must learn to chop a liver!"

If I were a rich Man

THE CHOSEN
EPISODE 3
BERNIE, WE'RE TRAVELLING TO THE PROMISED LAND. PREPARE FOR A DANGEROUS AND LONG JOURNEY. BRING A KNIFE.
REALLY? A KNIFE?
JUST A PRECAUTION
...I MIGHT MAKE A CHEESECAKE ALONG THE WAY!

Show us your profits!
Cor— Get your books out !!!
I'd like to take off your expenses against your income!!!
JEWISH ACCOUNTANTS AT WORK

"It" Hassidics

"Don't worry, they're harmless . . . they keep themselves to themselves!"

So........
Ruth tells me you're
a doctor !!!
No Mrs Weinstock, I'm
a **dotter**.........
I punch out the perforations
in toilet paper !

Yentas at dawn

Jewish TV advert from 1975
FAIRY
MUMMY, Why are your hands So Moist and shiny?

BECAUSE I'M PULLING THE KISHKES OUT OF THE CHICKEN!
SLOP!
SLOP!

YENTL
FLOSS

I ORDERED THE RIBEYE STEAK.... THIS IS THE RABBI STEAK!!!
SO???...WHAT DID YOU THINK OF THE SERVICE???

The Cavemans

"It's a very nice invention Laurence, but where do you put the cream cheese?"

"In the event of an emergency your life jacket can be found under your seat. It's the inflatable orange thing, although we do have it in a nice key-lime green, similar to the colour that Barbara Nershberg wore at the Glookman wedding!"

*"I'm sorry, it's just that . . . well, I'm Jewish and you're a builder . . .
we have nothing in common!!!"*

If the Waltons were Jewish . . .

This must be it Doctor Mcoy.... planet of the Yentas!
you're a doctor?

THE CHOSEN
EPISODE 4
CHILDREN OF ISRAEL, WE ARE IN TROUBLE, THERE IS NO MORE BREAD!
.....BUT WE MUST KEEP ON HOPING AND PRAYING, AND EVENTUALLY WE WILL FIND SOMETHING...
.....TO GO WITH THE HERRING AND FISHBALLS, AND EGG 'N' ONION!

"I just decided from a very early age that I was going to be a shmok!"

The Bronx 1920. When Jews ran the streets. I'm the notorious mob boss Bugsy Fishball, and these were some of the guys...
MITZY GLOOFMAN. IF HE SHRUGGED AT YOU.... OY !!!
'FISHLIPS' PEARLSKY. NOT NICE.
MORRY 'THE CHEESECAKE' SHNITZELPOTS. MONEY COLLECTOR FOR THE SHNEIDEL BOYS (CHARTERED ACCOUNTANTS)
FARVEL LIPSKY, RACKETEER, HITMAN, WEDDING CATERER.
LONGY SHORTMAN. (NOT LONG, NOT SHORT)
BIG BERNIE THE MESHUGGENAH. KING OF THE JEWISH UNDERWORLD. EVERYBODY WAS AFRAID OF BERNIE. ONCE KILLED 38 GUYS BECAUSE THEY WERE LOOKING AT HIS BAGEL.
SOLLY 'NO NOSE' KLOOMF. HIS NOSE GOT SHOT OFF, SO HE WORE A 'FALSIE'
WITZY "VIENNAS" YOTZELSHNAUB. HITMAN TURNED INFORMER. (TOLD HIS MOTHER EVERYTHING)
"THE BUTCHER". NO EXPLANATION REQUIRED. VERY VERY DANGEROUS.
"THE DENTIST" SPECIALIZED IN PAIN. (ACTUALLY, HE WAS JUST A LOUSY DENTIST.)

When Jewish immigrants first arrived in Britain over 100 years ago, one of the main problems they encountered was that they were all tailors.

"Erm . . . we've decided not to have the boy circumcised, Rabbi Shakeman!"

"I'm not sure about this new wailing wallpaper, Bernie!"

Zadie, we've been married for 60 years and there's something I have to tell you.... I've been faking it. I've never liked your chopped liver...... I find it too "bitty"!
sniff!
Have you been noshing someone else's behind my back?

A Jewish New Year's Resolution.....

I'M GIVING THESE DISGUSTING THINGS UP, BERNIE..... I HATE HAVING SUCH STINKY BREATH!

FAGS

AT LEAST I'LL STILL HAVE THE FAGS THOUGH!

FAGS

FISHBALLS

"Calm down honey!!! . . . why do you always get like this when Barry Manilow's on the radio???"

A Violent Scene from Jewish Brit-Gangster Movie
"LOKSHEN IN CHICKEN STOCK & TWO SMOKED HERRING BAGELS"
YOU SEE THIS GUN?... I CAN'T BELIEVE I'M HOLDING A GUN!!!... A JEWISH BOY LIKE ME! WITH A GUN!!! OY!!!
I KNOW!!! A GUN!!! OY OY OY!!!.... ...SO WHAT DOES IT DO?

Jewrobics

*". . . and shrug . . . and release . . . two three four . . .
and shrug . . . and release . . . and shrug . . ."*

Jewish Mafia threats.

Romeo and Juli-yenta

Advertisement

"Little Jewish Auntie"

A fine collector plate edged with 22 carat gold

A collector's treasure- a perfect gift

"Little Jewish Auntie" will be a beautiful addition to your home. It can be yours for just £3,985.00 (plus p+p)

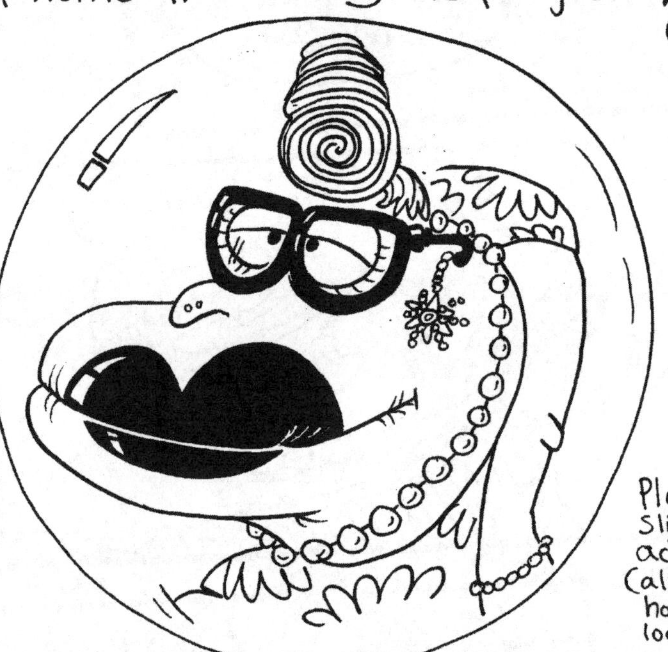

Plate shown slightly bigger than actual size (although it depends how closely you're looking at this page)

"I was delighted when my neighbour invited me to meet his little auntie," says artist Sheldon Moygul.....
"What an adorable little auntie, so lovely and affectionate, and her face held a hint of mischief......I just knew I would have to paint her!"

☐ Please charge my credit/debit card.
☐ Mastercard ☐ Visa/Delta

Card No: ☐☐☐☐☐☐☐☐☐☐☐☐☐☐☐☐

Card expiry date: ____________

Signature: ______________________

Pearl diving in Florida.

If I were a rich Man...

WE'VE KIDNAPPED
YOUR JEWISH AUNTIE.
PAY UP OR WE'LL.......
.....(WELL ACTUALLY,
FORGET THAT.......
JUST TAKE HER BACK...
PLEASE!!!)

WHO'D LIKE TO BE A
MILLIONAIRE
WHO'D LIKE TO BE A

YELDA POOPSKY FROM STAMFORD HILL, YOU DECIDED TO "PHONE A FRIEND"..... ...2½ HOURS AGO......
......SO I SAID TO HER, 'RENIE' I SAID, 'IF MELVIN WANTS TO WEAR THAT SHIRT, LET HIM, BUT NOT WHILE YOU'RE FRYING FISH IN THE HOUSE!..

Trouble at the OK already, my life . . .

"You got a broygus with me Ernie?"

"Okay, when I give the signal, I want you to have a ten-minute argument with me about who's supposed to be navigating!"

Y'KNOW, IT'S FUNNY. FOR TWO COMPLETE OPPOSITES, WE LOOK SO SIMILAR!
WE COULD BE BROTHERS!
SANTA

THE CHOSEN
EPISODE 5
OH GREAT— THE EGYPTIANS ARE CHASING US, AND WE'RE TRAPPED BY THE SEA!!!
DON'T WORRY. GOD WILL SAVE US!
RED SEA
HOW?
HE WILL PERFORM A MIRACLE!
RED SEA
WOW— THE WATER'S TURNED INTO WINE!!!
PSSST.... WRONG MIRACLE!
SORRY!
RED SEA

"There's something strange about your work Henry, and it's ever since you started eating those 'bagel' things!"

"All those in favour say 'Oy!!!'"

MADAM ZAZA
KNOWS ALL

MAUREEN
ZIMMERMAN
WANTS TO KNOW
EVERYTHING

THEATRE
IT'S BAD NEWS I'M AFRAID MR YOODLENIK, WE HAD TO AMPUTATE YOUR SHOULDER...........
...I'M AFRAID YOU MAY NEVER SHRUG AGAIN!
OY!!!

"Oy! Earthling . . . when I said 'take me to your leader' I didn't think it would be such a shlap!!!"

YIDDISHE STRIP BAR
I'M A "SHLAP-DANCER"... YOU PAY ME £10 AND I DANCE NAKED ON YOUR TABLE. BUT FIRST YOU HAVE TO LIFT ME UP ONTO THE TABLE!
10

SO YOU SEE, MY STRONG
RELIGIOUS BELIEFS DO NOT ALLOW
ME TO ENJOY SEX WITH MY WIFE.
.....WILL YOU BE MY WIFE?

SHMOCKBUSTER MOVIES TO RENT
Horror
My son's going out with a Gentile
SCARY !!!

"Honey, did you remember to let the Katz out?"

"DEAR MORRY,
I JUST GOT YOUR
MESSAGE IN THE
BOTTLE.....
SO YOU
COULDN'T
PHONE?!!!
YETTA xx"

"I decided to go for many colours this Autumn. I haven't actually done that with dreamcoats before, but hopefully it should get a lot of publicity!"

Jewish campfire stories

OH..... I THOUGHT YOU SAID THERE'S A HEAVY **'DEW'** ON THE GRASS!

"Great! . . . of all the tribes we could've come across, we had to run into the lost 'Meshuggenah people'!!!"

Jewish cannibals

And so surely the ancient writings of the prophets must teach us many things...
ooooohhh
...about our fathers before us, and their fathers before them. .
MMMM.:
...and we must continue these teachings to tomorrow's generations, so that they may go forth and teach their children. . . . .
oooh!
but let us stop now and get changed for aerobics.
(YES. . .)

THANK YOU FOR VISITING
EILAT
BAGGAGE
HALVA

"I wouldn't say my mother-in-law's fatty . . ."

From Roald Dahls' classic

Yenta and the Giant Peach

The Jazz Singer's father on holiday

FENG-SHUI

JEWISH FENG-SHUI

"Look honey . . . it's the Loch Ness Meshuggenah!!!"

Yiddishe 'ladies of the night'

JEWISH SEX AIDS
MY WIFE LIKES ME TO "DRESS UP"!
THIS IS THE RANGE!
NEIL DIAMOND OUTFIT
BARRY MANILOW OUTFIT
A DOCTOR

THE CHOSEN
EPISODE 6
LOOK SON, FERTILE LAND!
HOW CAN YOU TELL DAD?
LOOK AT THE BLOOMS!
....THEY'RE PICKING FLOWERS!
MORNING MR AND MRS BLOOM!
MORNING!

"Stand and chop liver!!!"

Why did the chicken cross the road?

IT'S DISGUSTING-
A KID
POSING
LIKE AN ADULT!!!
13 YEAR OLD
SUPERMODEL
JEREMY'S
BAR-MITZVAH
ALBUM

Jewish fairy tales

Isaac Newton discovers Judaism . . .

Macbeth Din

MUM, DAD,
THIS IS MY DATE IRVING.
IRVING'S A SHNORRER!
I'M NOT PAYING!!!

"I'm looking for Long John Silverman!"

According to ancient Jewish mythology, Oedipus Kleinman, unaware of his own identity, killed his father, and fell in love with his mother's cooking.

WHO'D LIKE TO BE A
MILLIONAIRE
WHO'D LIKE TO BE A

SHELDON GLIMSKY FROM HENDON.... FOR ONE MILLION POUNDS, A QUESTION ON DIY......
OY!

A Scene from George Orwell's *Kosher Animal Farm*

"So it's agreed then comrades . . . tomorrow we get rid of Farmer Cohen. I'll talk to my brother-in-law, Irwin the accountant, who'll draw up the papers!"

Although rarely mentioned in history books, it is now known that the Jewish Vikings were a particularly savage part of the eighth century, taking business cards and stealing clients from whichever country they invaded.

YIDDISHE SECTION
SH—
SHL-
SHM-
SHN—
SHT-

"The bad news is your son has swallowed a food blender. The good news is we can all have chopped liver!!!"

"Wow, what a coincidence . . . we both don't eat pork!!!"

IF I WERE A RICH MAN........

My daughter Yoitl wishes to marry Potsl the **sewage worker**...

THE CHOSEN FINAL EPISODE

And it came to pass that the Jewish people settled in the promised land, and built houses and cities and made the nation of Israel their home, despite being constantly at war with the aggressive neighbours.....

Brisman & sons
CIRCUMCISIONS
I'm sorry but we don't like to cut corners!

"Honey put some of this on . . . you don't want to burn!"

Before becoming a successful playwright, William Shakespeare began his career writing BarMitzvah speeches.

"Look Harry . . . Florida!!!"

How Picasso got started

"I like your style Pablo . . . but maybe you should think about branching out, and not just doing Bar Mitzvah portraits!"

Jewish nouvelle cuisine

Farmer Yitzy Pinkel, and his famous shmuckspreader.

"Son it's time you knew . . . we're not your real parents!"

"The examination shows you're not pregnant Mrs Shniffman, so I'm sending you down to the Excessive Noshing Department for some tests!"

Passover: A time for questions

everyone around me just seems TOO JEWISH!!!
Hmmm..... it's obviously making you very stressed! look at you..... you look so thin!..... maybe you should eat more. would you like some cheesecake?

Cohen Levi & Goldberg Ltd
fraud squad!

TONIGHT
JEWISH
PUB QUIZ
QUESTION 1: WHAT'S A PUB?
OY!
TAP TAP...
I'VE HEARD OF THEM...

"No Miss . . . the ladies is down the corridor!!!"